# Plant Parts

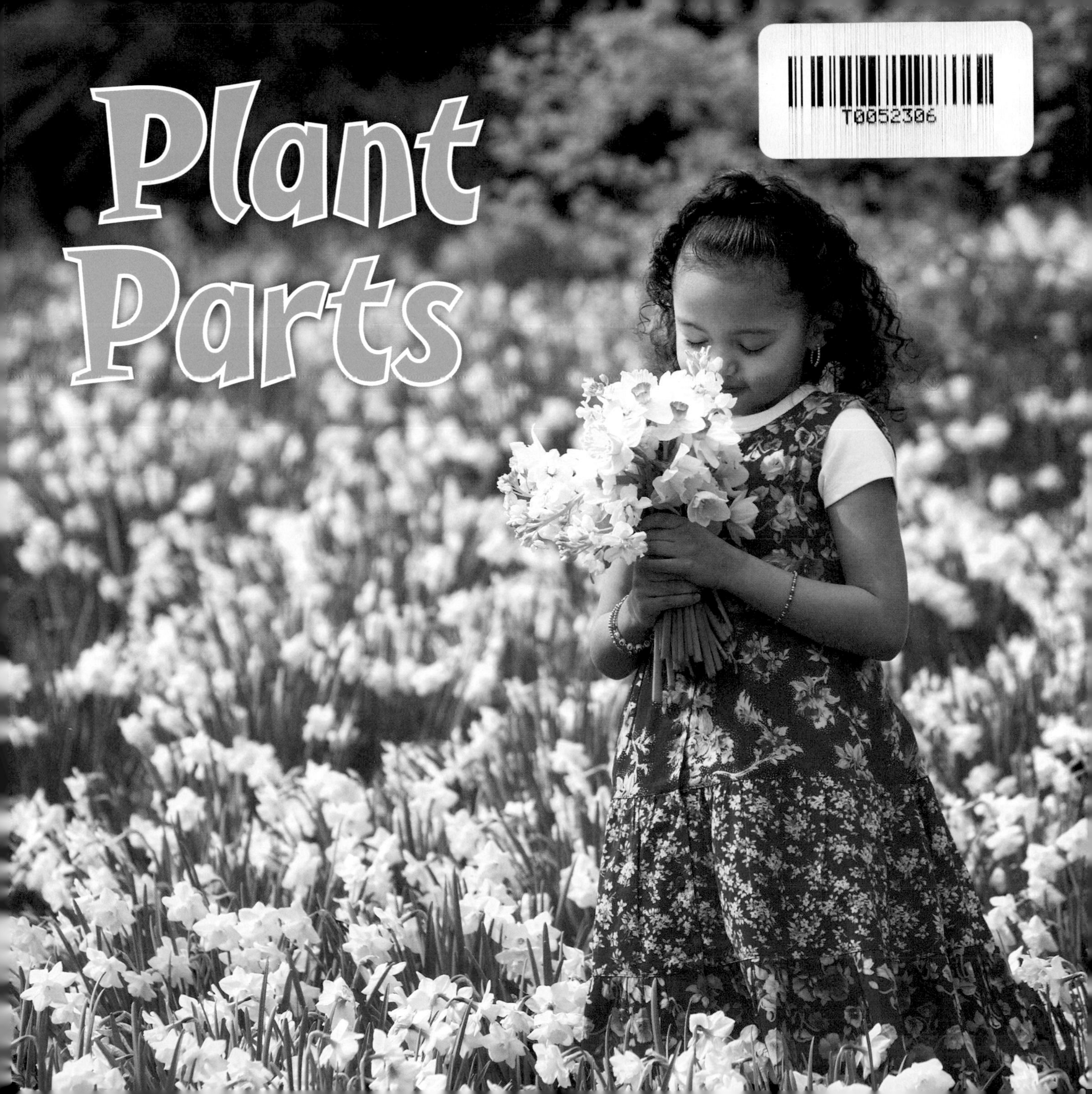

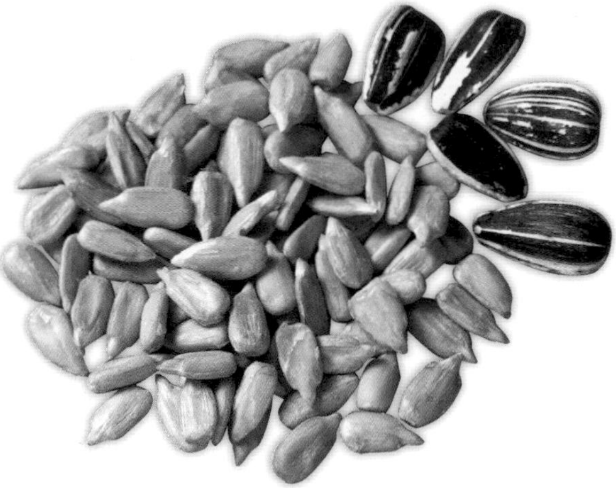

# seeds

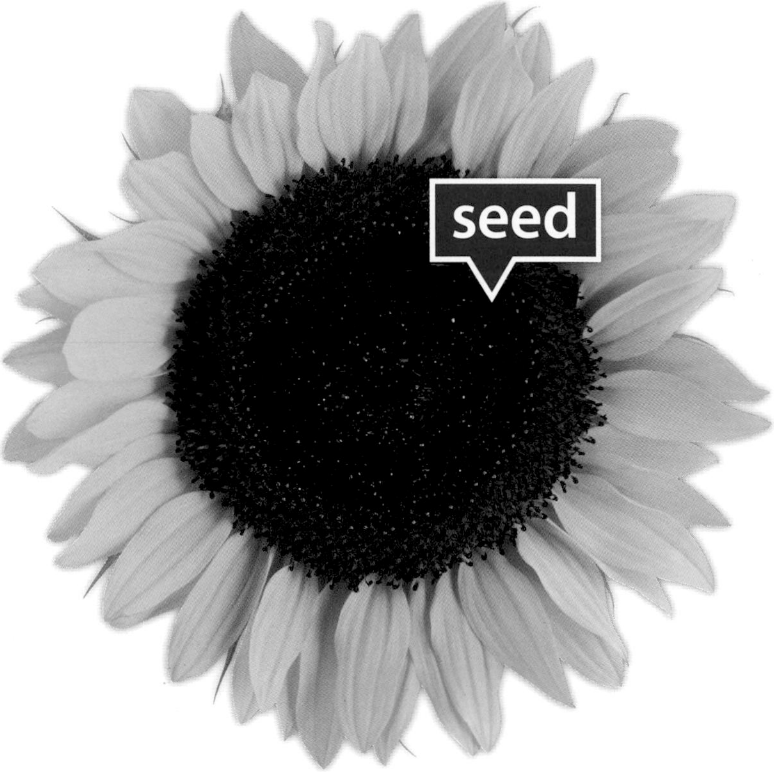

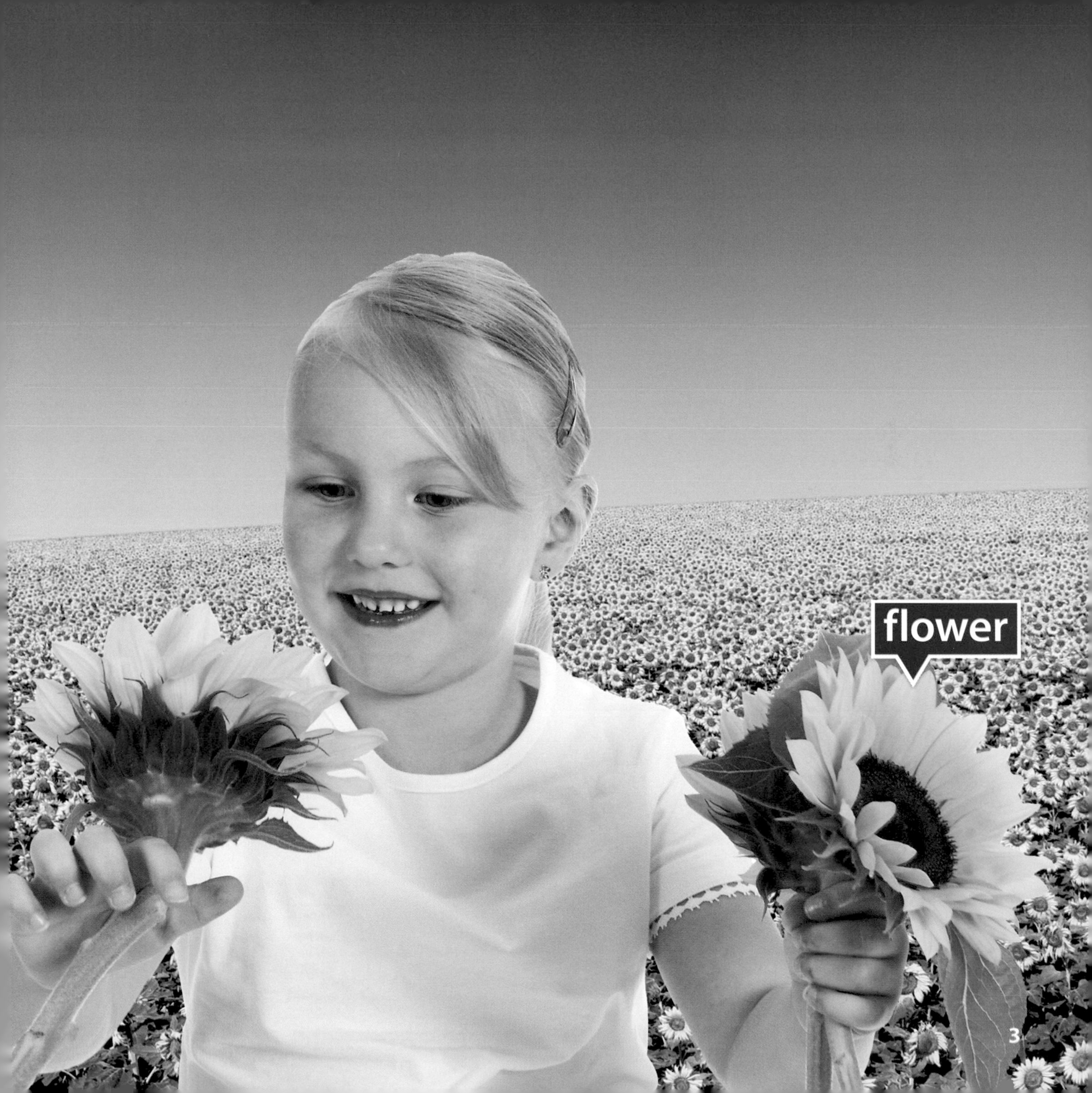
flower

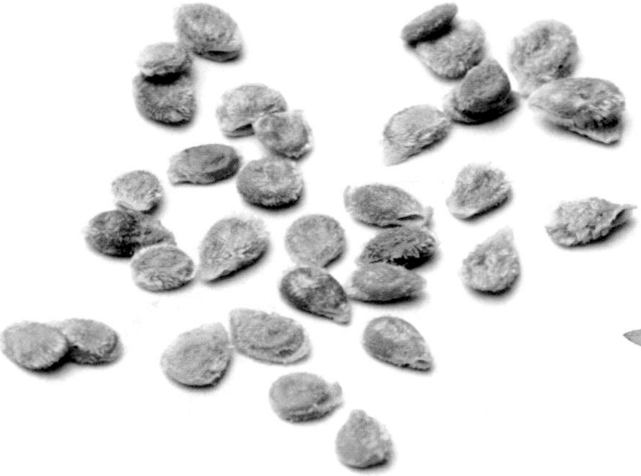

seeds

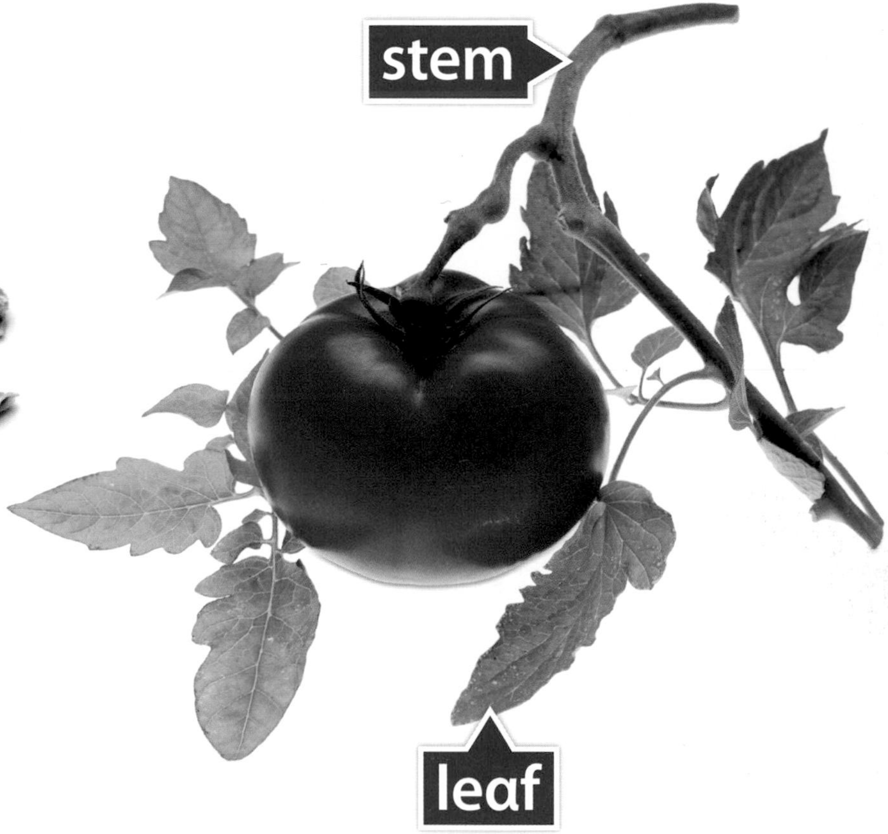

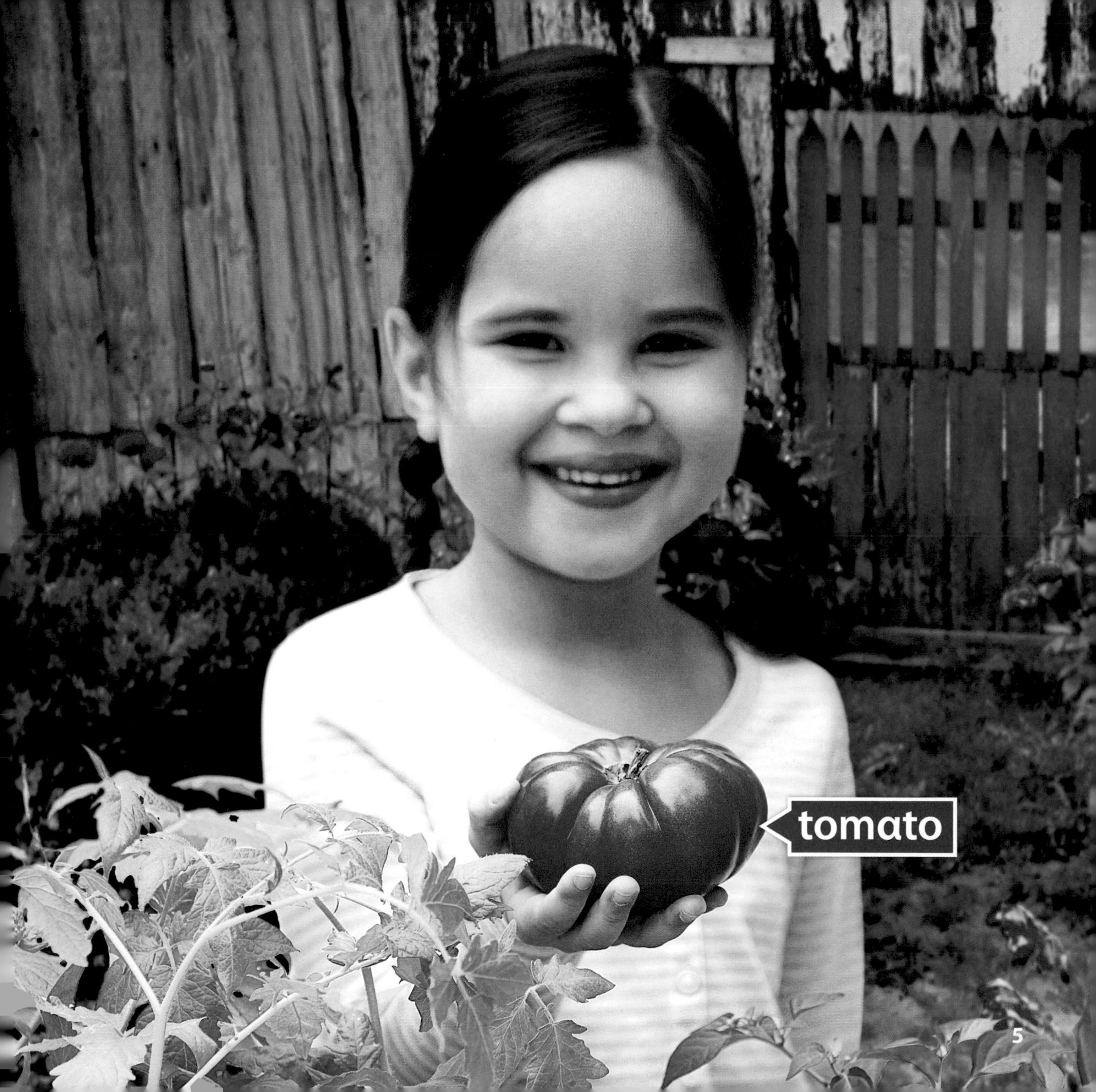
tomato

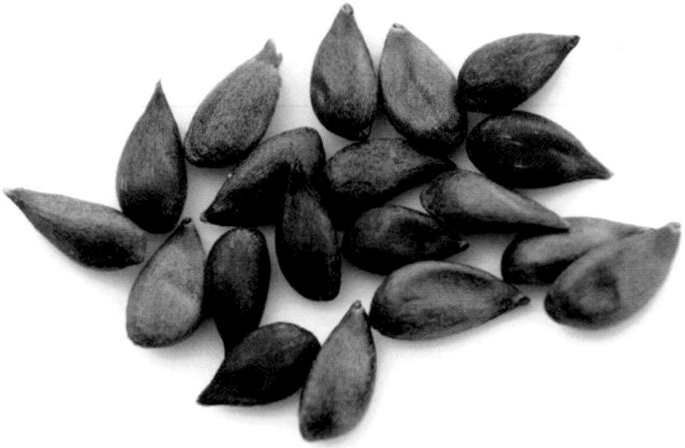

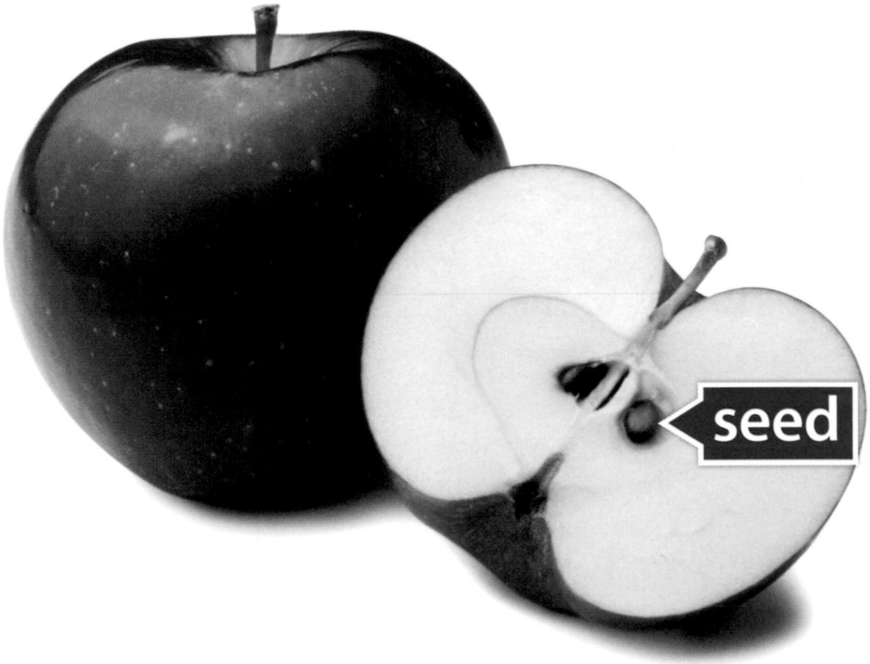


seeds

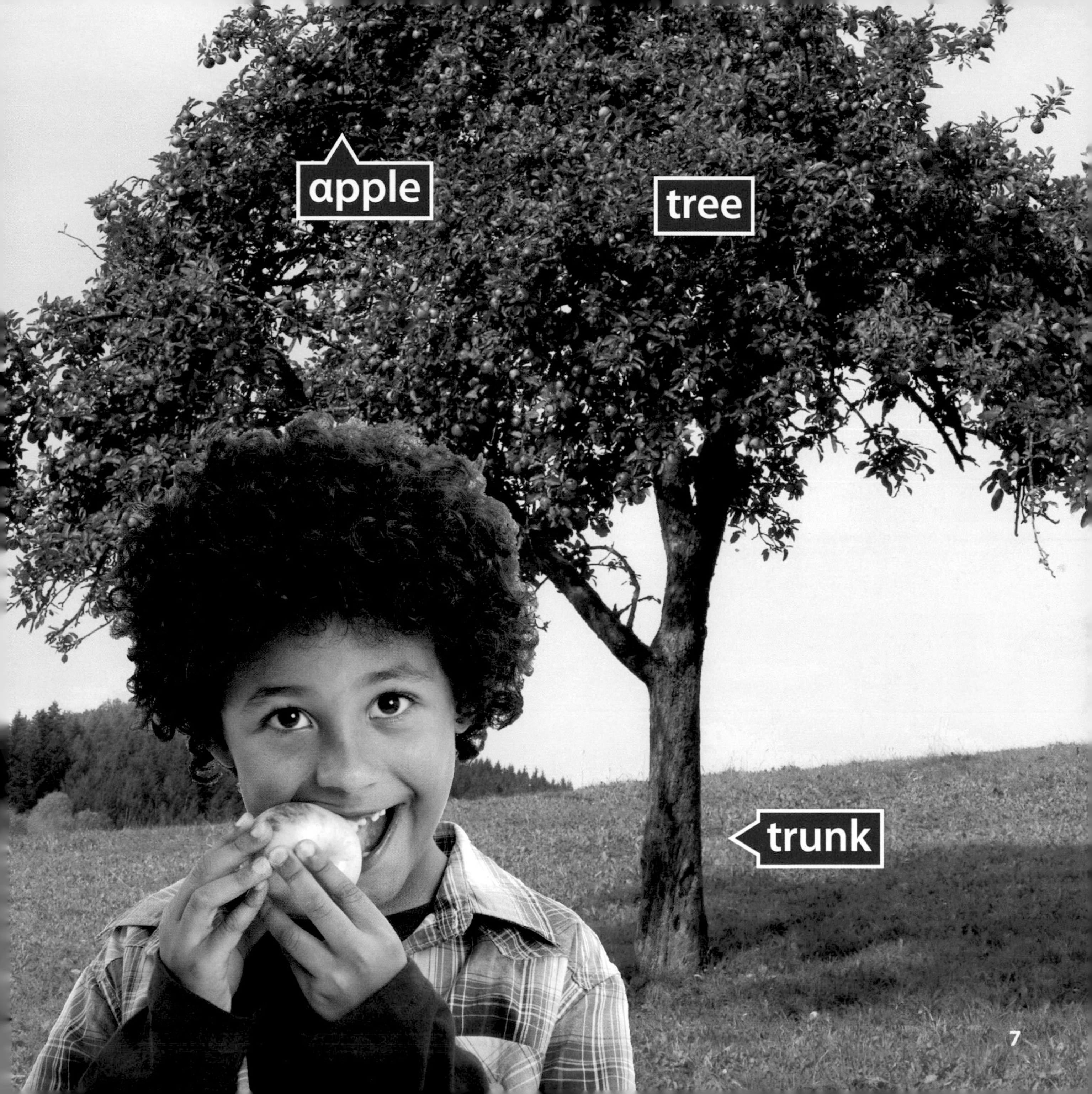
apple
tree
trunk

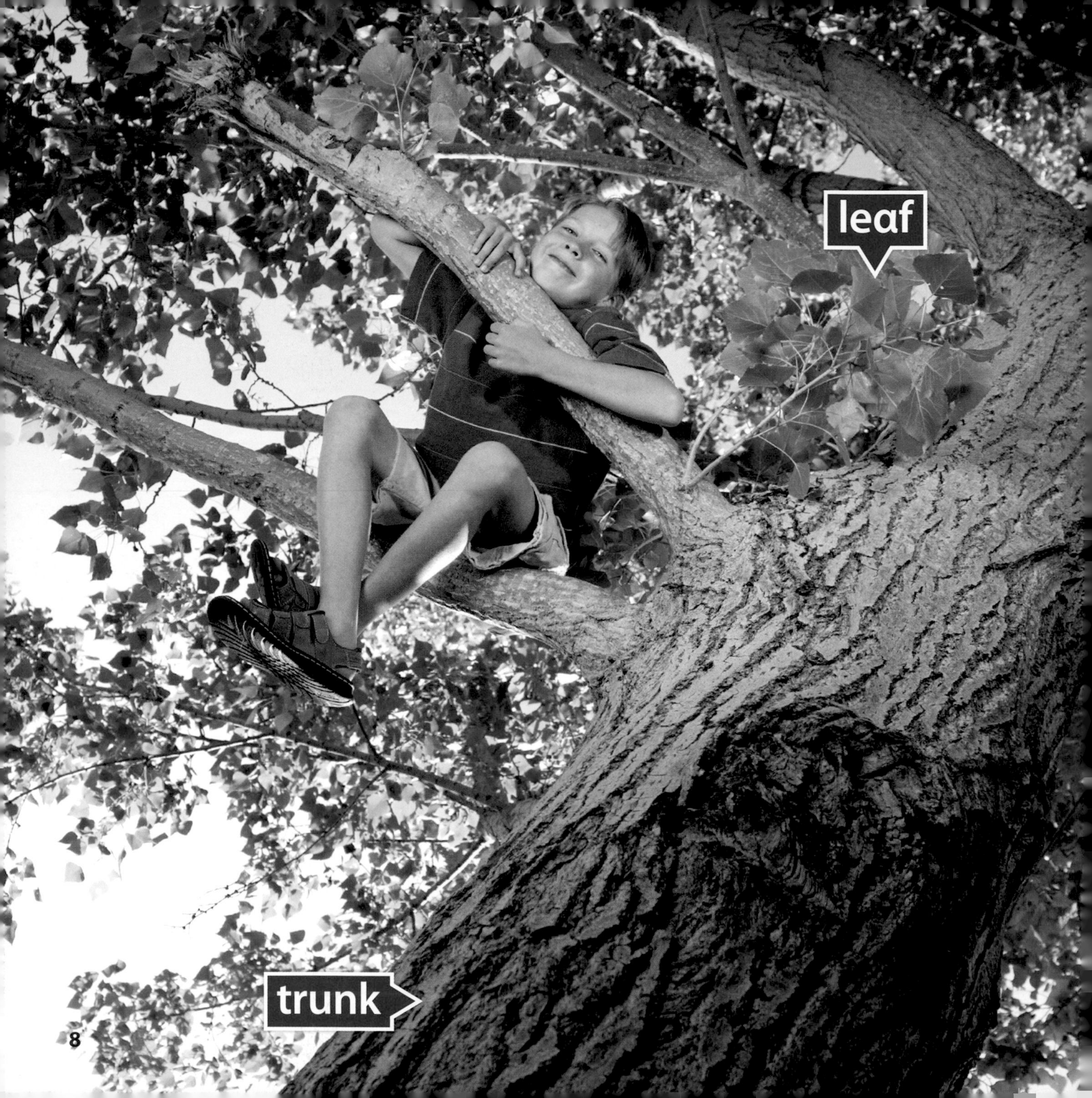
leaf
trunk